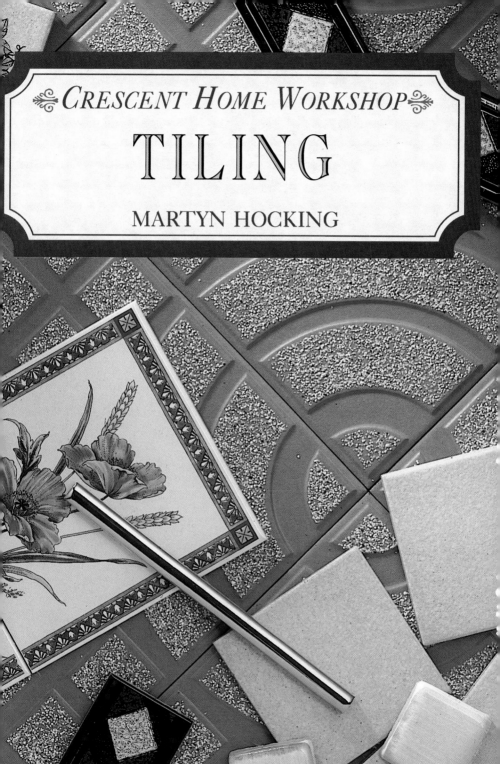

CRESCENT HOME WORKSHOP

TILING

MARTYN HOCKING

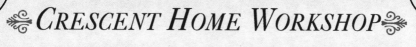

CRESCENT HOME WORKSHOP

TILING

MARTYN HOCKING

CRESCENT BOOKS
NEW YORK • AVENEL, NEW JERSEY

Home Workshop

TILING

Page 2:   Various types of relief, patterned, border, and edge-tiles.

This 1994 edition published by Crescent Books,
distributed by   Outlet Book Company, Inc.,
a Random House Company,
40 Engelhard Avenue, Avenel, New Jersey 07001

RANDOM HOUSE   New York • Toronto • London • Sydney • Auckland

Copyright © 1994   Harlaxton Publishing Limited
Copyright Design © 1994   Harlaxton Publishing Limited
2 Avenue Road, Grantham, Lincolnshire, NG31 6TA, United Kingdom.
A member of the Weldon International Group of Companies.

Publisher: Robin Burgess
Design and Coordination: Rachel Rush
Editing: Martyn Hocking
UPS Translations UK
Illustrator: Jane Pickering
Photography: Chris Allen, Forum Advertising Limited
Typesetting: Seller's, Grantham
Color Reproduction: GA Graphics, Stamford
Printing: Imago, Singapore

Title: Crescent Home Workshop - TILING
ISBN: 0-517-08780-4

CONTENTS

Clay tiles have been used in homes to cover walls and floors for thousands of years. From Roman times to the present day, they have been appreciated for their unique combination of durability and beauty.

While they are primarily used in kitchens and bathrooms, tiles can be used throughout the home and on a wide variety of surfaces.

Today, more materials than ever before are available in tile form – carpet, cushion vinyl, polystyrene, rubber, cork, and glass to name but six.

The growth of the home repair market has been largely responsible for this change. Tiles are considerably easier to lay than sheet materials and suit the inexperienced handyman.

But they have practical benefits too. You would never lay a roll of carpet in a kitchen, for fear of ruining it with a single spill. But you can lay carpet tiles in a kitchen, knowing that if one or two are spoiled, they can be quickly and inexpensively replaced.

While 'soft' tiles – carpet, vinyl, cork, rubber, and polystyrene – are particularly easy to work with, no tiling job should be beyond the capabilities of the amateur.

The key to achieving a good result in every case is careful preparation and planning. This book has been designed to guide you through this process.

OPPOSITE: Brightly-colored pieces of tile used in this mosaic give an added dimension to an otherwise plain wall.

Home Workshop
TILES AND TOOLS

There are literally thousands of different wall and floor tiles available – so how do you decide which ones will work best for you?

CHOOSING WALL TILES

Wall tiles are available in a vast range of styles and colors. They are made from a variety of materials in a limited number of sizes.

The vast majority of wall tiles are ceramic, with a smooth, glazed surface.

1: FIELD TILES – standards are the most common type. These have square edges, which need to be separated by spacers when laid. Field tiles (A) may have one (B), two (C), or all four edges glazed. The purpose of this edge-glazing is to allow tiles to be used at the tops of partly-tiled walls and on external corners where more than the face of the tile will be seen.

Tiles with no edge-glazing are still made and are suitable for plain walls, but border tiles will be needed to cover any exposed edges.

Field tiles are available in a range of sizes, but the most common are 4½in and 6in square. The standard thickness is 5/32in, but wall tiles are available up to a thickness of 3/8in. The latter are often reproductions of traditional 19th- and early 20th- century designs or 'rustic' imports from Mexico.

Some field tiles have small wings or 'lugs' on their edges to automatically create an even gap between them, doing away with the need for spacers.

A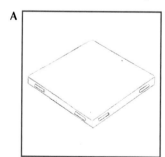

B

C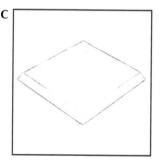

D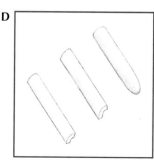

2: UNIVERSAL TILES – have angled rather than square edges, which are again designed to automatically create a regular gap between them. The most common sizes are 4$\frac{1}{2}$in square and 6in square, and glazing may extend over one, two or all four edges.

3: BORDER TILES – are available for use with field tiles which have unglazed edges. They are sometimes hard to find in the pattern and color you want and may have to be ordered rather than bought "off the shelf".

Border tiles with one rounded edge are traditionally known as bullnose tiles and are used along the top or side of a tiled panel. Tiles with two rounded edges are known as out-angle tiles and are used to form corners.

4: HEAT-RESISTANT TILES – are designed for use around cooking stoves and fireplaces. They are thicker than standard ceramic tiles to reduce the risk of cracking. All ceramic tiles have some degree of heat-resistance (none should crack in temperatures up to 100°C) thanks to the firing process they have undergone during manufacture.

5: EMBOSSED TILES – have a design molded into their surface and are used singly or in groups to create decorative patterns. In kitchen tile ranges, they often feature cooking motifs. In bathrooms, the designs often have a nautical flavor.

Embossed tiles may be the same size as the plain field tiles around them but can also be found in 6in x 2in or 4$\frac{1}{2}$in x 2in strips for use in horizontal rows.

2

6: DADO TILES – are specially shaped to resemble the wooden dado rails used in traditional drawing-rooms to protect walls from chair and sofa backs. In hallways, bathrooms, and kitchens their use is purely decorative, to cap a part-tiled wall.

7: MOSAIC TILES – are small ceramic chips held together by a backing material. This backing material automatically creates even spacing between the tiles. The chips are usually $3/4$in to 1in square, but hexagons and other shapes are also available (see page 17).

The backing sheets are made from string, paper, or nylon. In some cases, the chips are held together by a paper facing that is soaked off once the tiles are in place (see page 26). Sheets are generally 12in square.

8: CERAMIC TRIMS – are designed to fill gaps around the edges of baths and kitchen worktops. Bathtub and shower trims are quadrant in shape and can be fixed in placed using a silicone sealant that will flex with the tub or shower when it is in use. Worktop trims are L-shaped and are fixed in place before the rest of the tiles (see D, page 8).

3

There are a number of alternatives to ceramic.

CORK TILES – are invariably 12in x 12in square. They can give a room a warm appearance for relatively little expenditure. Covering walls with cork is a quick way to hide slightly uneven or stained surfaces, but is no cure for dampness.

Both cork and polystyrene tiles will help to insulate a cold room. The latter have been used extensively in the past to cover an uneven ceiling. They are not suitable for use in kitchens for reasons of fire safety.

Covering a wall with mirror-glass tiles is an effective way to make a small room appear more spacious.

BRICK SLIPS – are thin strips of masonry which can be attached to a plain wall to imitate the appearance of plain brickwork. They are often used to cover chimney breasts, breakfast bars, and pillars.

5
6

NEXT PAGE: Rustic terracotta combined with ethnic influenced patterns make an attractive border in this bathroom.

TILING TOOLS

There are a number of inexpensive hand-tools available to cut and shape tiles. You will need these to cut tiles around pipes and bathroom fittings and to fit tiles around the edges of the room.

1: ADHESIVE SPREADER – a plastic card with a notched leading edge. Helps to ensure an even spread of adhesive across the wall or floor. These are often supplied with tubs of adhesive.

2: CHINAGRAPH PENCIL – to mark the glazed surface of a tile to show your cut line.

3: FLOOR SCRIBER – a marking tool you can make yourself from an offcut of wood

4: GAUGE-STICK – a useful tool you can make yourself from a strip of wood. A gauge-stick will help you decide how best to arrange your tiles so that there are no ugly slivers at either end of a row. To make one, simply place the stick on the floor and lay a line of tiles out along it, complete with spacers. Mark the corners of each tile on the stick in pencil.

5: HOLE-SAW – a special type of hole-saw with tungsten-carbide teeth will be useful if you have to cut a tile to fit around a large diameter pipe.

6: PLUMB BOB – a metal weight attached to a length of string which will help you to make sure your first tile column is vertical.

7: PROFILE-GAUGE – this is useful for shaping around awkward objects to work out how to cut the tile to fit around them.

8: SPIRIT LEVELS – are essential pieces of equipment. Tiles are meant to be laid in straight lines and any appreciable deviation from this norm will spoil the finished effect. Check every tile you lay with a pocket-size level both horizontally and vertically. A full-length level will be needed to check rows and columns.

9: TILE CUTTER – there are a number of versions available, but all of them do basically the same three jobs – they measure off the amount of tile you want to remove on a plastic gauge; score along the cutting line with a tungsten-carbide wheel; and then snap the tile along this line using strong leveraged jaws.

> **Cheaper hand-held versions may not offer a measuring facility and will require you to provide rather more of the leverage.**

10: TILE-DRILL – a drill-bit with a spear-shaped tip to make holes in glass and ceramic tiles without shattering them. An essential tool to fix closets or shelves to a tiled surface.

11: TILE FILE – an inexpensive strip of metal lattice coated with tungsten-carbide particles. Ideal for smoothing off rough fragments and forming curves along the edges of tiles that have been cut roughly to shape with nibblers.

> **Tile-files can also be used to shave a fraction or two off the side of a tile that has been very slightly under-cut, but this is hard work.**

If you have misjudged the size of the gap you are trying to fill by more than this amount, cut a fresh tile. You will probably find a use for the oversized one elsewhere in the room.

Some tilers prefer to use a carborundum stone for filing work. These are more durable than metal lattices, but are also more expensive.

12: TILE NIPPERS – pincers with hardened teeth. As the name suggests, these are used to nip small sections of tile away to fit around an awkward obstacle like a doorframe or pipe. A pair of nippers is not a precision instrument in the hands of the amateur and should only be used for rough shaping work. Always use a file to finish the job.

> **A pair of heavy-duty nippers will be needed to shape thicker tiles, even then the going can be tough. A pair of work-gloves offers your hands a measure of protection.**

13: TILE SAW – a hacksaw fitted with a tungsten-carbide-coated blade. The ideal tool for cutting awkward curves and other intricate shapes. Far less effective, though, on thicker tiles, where a lot of elbow power will be required. Produces a much finer finish than a pair of nippers, but you will still need to smooth edges with a file.

14: TILE SNAPPER – a tool that looks like a pair of pliers, but with one tip flattened and the other set at right angles to it. Place your scored tile in its jaws with the cut line positioned in the center, then squeeze. The tile should break along the cut line.

> **Snappers are for breaking tiles of a specific thickness, according to brand. Heavy-duty tiles must be split with a substantial tile cutter.**

15: TILE SPACERS – it is important to leave a gap between one tile and the next to allow for any slight movement in the wall or floor. Without these gaps, the tiles would bulge and crack under the pressure. The size of gap you leave is a matter of personal taste, but again symmetry is critical and spacers make this a lot easier to achieve.

Plastic spacers are inexpensive, but you may prefer to use spent matchsticks, or even strips of cardboard. Many modern tiles have edges shaped to create this gap automatically without the need for spacers.

16: TILE SPIKE OR SCORER – a tool used for marking the cut line on the surface of a tile. This creates a weak point along which the tile should snap cleanly. Used in combination with a snapper as an alternative to an all-in-one tile cutter.

TILING ADHESIVES

There are a number of different adhesives available for fixing tiles to the various surfaces around the home. For this reason, it is important to read the manufacturer's instructions carefully when choosing an adhesive.

If you are tiling around a shower area, for example, it is essential to choose a waterproof adhesive. If you are tiling around a stove, a heat-resistant adhesive will be needed.

OPPOSITE: Mosaic tiles attached to a backing sheet that maintains an even spacing for the grout.

Home Workshop

TILING WALLS

Tiling walls is all about planning – if you start in the right place and can follow a pattern you should not go wrong.

BELOW: Practical but attractive country style tiles are perfect for storage areas.

WHERE TO START TILING

There are two points to consider when deciding where to start. Firstly, there is the need to get your first row of tiles as near to horizontal as you can, and secondly, the need to avoid fitting tiny slivers of tile at either end of all subsequent rows and columns.

Do not make the mistake of assuming that your base-board will naturally be level because it is in contact with the floor. The floor will almost certainly have a slope.

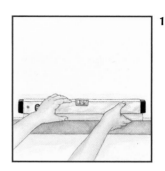

1 The way to guarantee that you are starting from a level plane is to make your own, using a wooden batten nailed lightly to the wall just above the baseboard. The size of your tiles will determine roughly how far above you fix it – with 6in tiles the gap between the top of the batten and the top of the baseboard should be around 4in-5in.

You will lay your first row of tiles along the top of this batten.

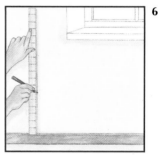

2 Gravity dictates that your horizontal guide batten should be fixed at the bottom of the wall rather than the top. It is a lot easier and quicker to slide tiles in subsequent rows down into position rather than pushing them up from below. If you started tiling at the top of a wall and worked down-ward, you would waste a lot of time re-positioning tiles that had slipped or sagged out of line.

3 You should use your gauge-stick to avoid having to fit tiny slivers of tile around the edges of the room.

4 A professional tiler will spend an hour or more sizing up the room in this way before starting work and you would be well-advised to do the same. You will need to consider every surface and obstacle, every window and doorway.

5 If you have never tiled before, it is a good idea to start in an unobtrusive corner of the room to build up your confidence for using spacers and adhesive. This is fine, but you must still plan the rest of the job thoroughly before that first tile goes up.

6 The best way to do this is to actually mark the wall with a pencil to show where each row of tiles will be fixed. This will quickly show you if you are going to have an awk-ward gap to fill under a window or over a bathtub and allow you to adjust your starting point without wasting materials.

TILING A PLAIN WALL

1

2

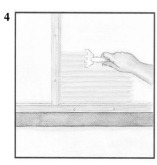

4

Once you have marked out your wall and are happy that your starting point takes account of all the obstacles you are going to encounter, you are ready to fit your horizontal batten. A piece of 2in x 1in timber is ideal, but the size is not critical.

1 Nail one end of the batten to the wall at your chosen height, taking care not to drive the head right in. That is because you are going to want to remove this batten later without disturbing the tiles above it.

2 Use your spirit level to establish a horizontal, and nail the other end of the batten in place. If your batten is going to stretch along the whole wall, you will find a second pair of hands useful. If you cannot run a single batten along the entire wall because there are obstructions, use two or three shorter ones that are all correctly aligned.

Walls are no more certain to be vertical than floors are horizontal, so you will need to fit a second guide batten to the wall to keep your columns straight.

3 Nail a second batten at right angles to the first in the corner where you have chosen to start work. Like your horizontal batten, this one should be fixed to the wall approximately two-thirds of a tile's width in from the edge of your tiling surface. Again, do not drive the nails right into the wall as they will need to be removed later.

4 Use a notched spreader to cover an area of wall two or three square feet immediately above your horizontal batten with adhesive. Do not cover an area any larger than this or there is a risk that the adhesive will have started to set before you have laid all the tiles. Aim to apply just sufficient adhesive so that no part of the wall behind is visible. The spreader will create ridges in the adhesive to improve the grip on the back of the tile, which will itself generally have a ribbed back.

5 Applying adhesive to the wall rather than the back of each tile individually saves time, ensures a more even thickness, and makes each tub of glue go a lot further. You will inevitably spread far more adhesive on the back of each tile if you 'butter' them individually than you would do working the other way around.

6 Lay half a dozen tiles along the top of the batten, inserting spacers between them if necessary. As you press each tile against the wall, give it a twist to the left and right to spread the adhesive evenly over the back of the tile. Then carefully slide it into its final position. If you do not give it a twist, the tile will almost certainly slip a fraction of an inch down the wall as you release it.

7 Double-check that each tile is level once you have positioned it. You will find a bullet/torpedo spirit level the most convenient tool for doing this.

8 Try to make sure that you wipe any traces of adhesive off the face of the tiles with a damp cloth before it dries. It will still be possible to remove spots of glue after it has set with the aid of a trimming knife, but you will risk scratching the surface of the tiles in doing so.

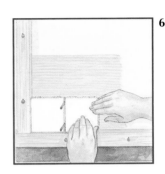

6

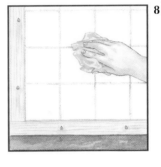

8

GROUTING

Grouting stops dirt and mold building up in the gaps between the tiles. To do its job effectively, grouting must be pressed firmly into place.

Some grouts are sold in powder form and have to be mixed with water. Others are sold ready-mixed. If you are tiling around a shower that will regularly get soaked, use a special epoxy-based waterproof grout.

Grouting should not be applied for at least eight hours after tiling, to allow the adhesive to set. In practical terms, this means an overnight break in the work.

Special tools are available for applying grout, but the back edge of an adhesive spreader will also do the job. Many people find a sponge a useful tool for this purpose. A professional will use a special squeegee, but you will probably find this relatively difficult to use for forcing the grout into the gaps.

Concentrate on getting a liberal amount of grout into the gaps initially – the excess can be removed quite easily with a damp cloth or sponge.

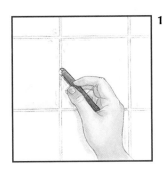

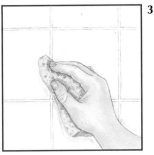

1 You can buy a special tool to smooth over the surface of the grout, but this can be done just as effectively with a piece of doweling or the blunt end of a pencil.

2 Draw your smoothing tool towards you – never push it away or it may dig in and dislodge some of the grout.

3 When the grout has dried, you will inevitably find traces on the surface of the tiles themselves. Remove these with a clean, dry cloth, which can be used to polish the surface of the wall.

OPPOSITE: Simple, pretty, textured tiles used in effective repeating-block arrangements.
NEXT PAGE: Striking tiled walls and practical floors in a contemporary kitchen.

APPLYING MOSAIC TILES

Mosaic tiles are designed to be quick and easy to apply but there are a couple of points to watch.

Take great care to maintain a consistent grouting gap when you are butting one sheet of tiles up to another. The perfect symmetry of the rest of the grouting will throw any deviation here firmly into the spotlight. Tiles with a front paper covering need to be grouted prior to hanging:

1 Lay the sheets face down on your workbench and apply a coat of grout with a spreader.

2 Let this dry for five minutes while you are spreading adhesive over the wall.

3 Hang the sheets of tiles on the wall with the paper covering facing toward you.

4 Leave to dry overnight, then soak the paper off with a little warm water. If you get the entire surface moist, the paper should peel off in one go.

5 Apply fresh grout to any bare patches between the tiles.

TILING INTERNAL CORNERS

You will almost invariably have to cut both tiles to form the angle at an internal corner. When you are planning the job, try to ensure that you cut about the same amount off each tile to achieve a balanced appearance.

Overlap the tiles in the corner so as to hide the cut edges. Leave a standard grout gap between the tiles to allow for any movement between the walls.

As soon as you have laid two or three tiles on the return wall, stretch your long spirit level across the corner of the room to check that you are still working on the same horizontal plane.

TILING EXTERNAL CORNERS

At an external corner, overlap the tiles so that you see the full face of the one that is on the prominent wall.

If you have to cut this tile, fix it in place with the cut edge hidden by grouting and the uncut edge on the corner where the glazing can be seen.

OPPOSITE: Corners and edges are accentuated here using the pretty, fresh design of these tiles.

TILING AROUND A WINDOW

1

If the room to be tiled has a window, it is likely to be one of the focal points, so it is important that the tiles here fit together well.

You may decide, for example, that you would like the row fixed to the wall just below the window to consist of whole tiles. In this case, you will need to adjust your starting point accordingly. A gauge-stick should make the task of marking out the wall fairly straightforward.

1 If you opt for whole tiles here, these should overlap the edge of the window bay by the thickness of one tile. This will allow you to butt the strips of tile laid inside the recess up against them to form a right-angle.

2 All the tiles fitted in the recess, both horizontally and vertically, must be carefully aligned with those on the adjoining walls.

3 You may also decide that you want to make the center of the window bay a focal point. In the planning phase, it would be worth marking the wall midway between the two sides of the bay and laying tiles out from this point to the walls. You may find that this leaves you with an awkward gap to fill at one or both ends, in which case your starting point will have to be adjusted. The important thing is to explore all the possibilities before you start tiling.

CUTTING TILES TO FIT AROUND BATHROOM FITTINGS

If you are decorating a bathroom which already has the basin and toilet in place, you will almost certainly have to cut and shape tiles to fit.

1 A profile gauge – a measuring device consisting of a row of sliding pins held between two handles – will help here. Press the gauge against the edge of the obstacle and mold the pins to its outline.

2 Transfer this outline onto the front of the tile to be cut, using a chinagraph pencil. Make sure you keep the sides of the gauge square to the sides of the tile as you do this.

3 Cut out the waste portion of the tile using a tile saw (for tiles up to 5/32in thick) or a pair of heavy-duty nippers.

It is always a good idea (especially if you are using nippers) to leave a 1/16in or so of waste on the tile. Check the fit against the obstacle to ensure your measurement was accurate before going any further.

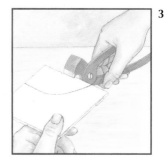

4 Nip off any rough spots and then smooth the edge of the tile with a file.

5 It may be more convenient, in this instance, to apply the adhesive to the back of the tile rather than the wall.

6 Any gap between the edge of the tile and the obstacle should be filled with a flexible silicone sealant that will allow for movement between the two in the future. A tub filled with warm water, for example, will flex outward quite considerably in use, and quickly crack a conventional filler.

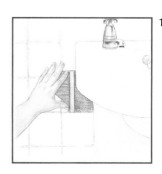

Use flexible filler in earthquake zones for all your tiles, to allow for vibration or movement from minor quakes.

CUTTING TILES TO FIT AROUND PIPES

2

5

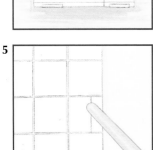

Cutting a tile to fit around a pipe can appear an awkward task, but it is quite simple once you know how.

In most bathrooms you have to cut at least one tile to fit around a water supply pipe.

1 Start by drawing a vertical line down the front of the tile, using a chinagraph pencil. The line should pass through the center of where the pipe will be when the tile has been fixed to the wall. Mark the point on this line where the pipe will pass through the tile.

2 Split the tile in two along the line and then lay the two halves side-by-side on your work surface. Then take a small round object (a coin will do) and trace its outline on the two tile halves to mark where the pipe will go. The object you choose should be about $1/16$in larger in diameter than the pipe.

3 Use a tile-scorer to etch this outline into the surface of the tile to encourage a clean break. Then remove the waste with a pair of nippers.

4 File the rough edges of both semicircles using abrasive paper wrapped around a pencil – a tile-file will be too big and awkward to insert here.

5 Spread the back of both parts of the tile with adhesive and ease them into position around the pipe.

Cutting large diameter holes to accommodate waste pipes can be tackled in a different way if you are able to disconnect the section of pipe that passes through the outside wall. A tungsten-carbide toothed hole-saw is the all-important tool here.

A hole-saw is a short saw-blade curled into a round metal frame that fits onto the end of an electric drill.

It is important to choose one designed for cutting tiles – ordinary hole-saws are used on wood and their teeth will only scratch the surface of a ceramic tile. If you do not want to buy one, these special hole-saws are available for rent from rental stores at minimal cost.

DRILLING HOLES IN TILES

If you wish to hang mirrors, storage units and other items from your newly-tiled walls, you will need to use a special drill-bit to make the holes for any fixings.

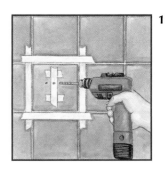

1

A tile/glass drill-bit has a tip that has been shaped to reduce the risk of cracking. It can be used with either an electric or a hand drill (use a hand drill, not an electric drill, when making holes in glass).

1 Prevent the drill-bit slipping on the smooth tile surface by sticking a piece of masking tape over the spot where the hole is going to be made.

2 If you are using an electric drill, set it at a low speed to minimize vibration. Drill through to the wall behind.

3 When you are attaching the fixing, take care not to over-tighten the screw, as this could crack the tile.

BELOW: Simple and effective use of textures and colors to create a rustic look in a modern bathroom.

'Avignon-Vert': Pilkingtons

REMOVING DAMAGED TILES

A tile that has been chipped or damaged in some other way can be replaced fairly easily. The important thing is to do this without damaging any of the bordering tiles.

4

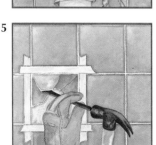

1 Wear plastic goggles and gloves for this job to protect yourself against sharp flying fragments of tile.

2 Tape the damaged tile area around the outside edge. Place a strip of tape near the center of the tile to prevent the drill bit from slipping on the glazed surface.

3 Make a hole in the middle of the damaged tile using an electric drill that has been fitted with a masonry bit.

4 Enlarge this hole with an old chisel, drive the blade at an angle, striking the back of the handle with a hammer.

5

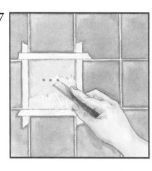

5 As fragments of tile split, pull them away with your hands. Take care at the edges not to work the chisel blade under any neighboring tiles as this will loosen them.

6 When you have removed the whole tile, you will be left with a patch of wall covered in ridges of old adhesive. While this can be chipped away with the chisel blade, you can get the job done a lot more quickly using a hot-air gun.

7 Heat the blade of a metal scraper and then use this to strip off the old adhesive. Do not apply heat directly to the adhesive as this may crack the adjoining tiles.

7

8 Lightly smear adhesive over the back of the new tile with a notched spreader and press it against the wall. You may need to use strips of cardboard to wedge it into place until the adhesive has partially set.

9 Leave the repair to dry overnight before grouting.

8

Floor tiles need to be more hardwearing than wall tiles, with the added requirement that when they become wet they must not become slippery to walk on.

CHOOSING FLOOR TILES

CERAMIC TILES – are the most durable option, being fired to such a high temperature during manufacture that the clay particles actually fuse together. They are available in a wide range of colors and patterns. Floor tiles are thicker (typically $1/2$in) and larger (typically 10sq in) than wall tiles.

Do not use wall tiles on a floor – they will be prone to cracking and the glazed surface will be too smooth to walk on safely when wet. Ceramic tiles are more likely to crack in earthquake zones.

SLATE AND STONE TILES – are other options if you are looking for a solid, hardwearing floorcovering. Both are expensive but offer a natural finish that cannot be matched by mass production methods.

Neither material is particularly easy to cut using home handyman tools and you may prefer to hire a professional to do the work.

At the other end of the price scale, vinyl and cork tiles are simple to lay and will provide a warm and comfortable surface on which to walk. Neither will last as long as a hard floor-covering, but their price reflects this fact.

1   CORK FLOOR TILES – contain a higher percentage of wood than cork wall tiles which makes them more durable. Check the packaging labels to ensure that you have the right kind.

2   VINYL TILES – are available in a range of thicknesses – generally, thicker tiles will last longer.

CARPET TILES – offer the warmth and comfort of wall-to-wall carpeting with the convenience of a covering that can be replaced in sections should it be damaged by burns or stains.

RUBBER TILES – were originally made for use in offices but look good in a modern home. They usually have a dimpled finish to improve grip and are available in plain colors.

NEXT PAGE:
The use of a contrasting bordered panel adds another dimension to an otherwise plain floor.

'Pastiche', 'Geometric' and 'Bistro Caraway'. Finishing Touches. Heuga.

PREPARING SOLID FLOORS FOR TILING

2

It is essential to prepare the entire floor area thoroughly before you start tiling.

Solid concrete floors can accept all types of floor tile but must be both dry and level. A newly-laid concrete floor should be left for at least a month to dry out completely.

1 Prime the floor surface using a diluted polyvinyl acetate adhesive applied with an old paintbrush.

2 Fill minor dents and cracks using a fine sand-and-cement screed. When this has dried, fill the damaged area using a mix of one part cement to three parts sharp sand. Add just enough water to bind the two together, plus a little adhesive.

3

3 A gently-sloping floor or one that is deeply cracked or pitted will need to be completely re-surfaced, using a self-levelling compound. You can check the gradient of a slope with the aid of a spirit level and a batten that is long enough to stretch right across the room. Wedge the batten at the foot of the slope until the spirit level registers horizontal. If the fall across the room is more than 1/2in, you will need to apply a full screed (see page 44).

4 A self-levelling compound must be applied to a clean, grease-free surface to achieve a good contact. Brush dirt out of recesses or cracks and then wash the floor with warm, soapy water. Mix the compound in a bucket following the manufacturer's instructions; making sure there are no lumps.

5

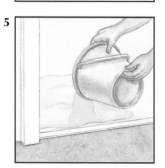

5 Pour the compound over the floor, starting in the corner furthest from the door. Use a steel float to spread the compound evenly over the surface. Any lumps or marks on the surface can be smoothed off with the float and a little water when the floor has dried out.

A sand-and-cement screed can be used to level a very uneven floor where a self-leveling compound cannot be used. In such cases, tiles can be laid directly onto the wet cement screed immediately after it has been laid (see page 44).

You do not need to remove old floor tiles if they are firmly attached – simply lay the new tiles over the top. If the tiles are very uneven but resist attempts to pry them up, apply a self-leveling compound over them first.

Home Workshop

PREPARING WOODEN FLOORS FOR TILING

Wooden floorboards that are in good condition can support the heaviest ceramic tiles, but first need to be covered with chipboard or plywood to create an even and consistent subsurface.

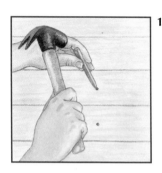

1 Examine the floor on your hands and knees, hammering down any protruding nail heads and fixing loose boards back in place with special nails called cut floor brads.

2 Before you cover the boards, make sure that you will be able to gain access to any pipes or wiring beneath them from adjoining rooms.

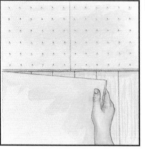

3 Use 1/2in thick chipboard or plywood to cover the floor-boards – anything thinner will be too flexible. Nail the sheets down at 1/2in intervals right across the room, taking care to sink each nail head below the surface with a nail punch. This is especially important when laying soft floor-coverings, as the slightest bump will show – and eventually wear through. Use nails that are long enough to penetrate the floorboards without going through them into any pipes or wires below.

Once the tiles have been laid, you will not be able to get at them directly without spoiling your new surface. If you are unsure on this point, ask a professional to take a look before you proceed.

Home Workshop
LAYING FLOOR TILES

A ll floor tiles are laid in basically the same way, whether they are made of slate or soft cushion vinyl. The only exception is for tiles you are laying them on a wet sand-and-cement screed (see page 44).

BELOW: Soft pink carpet tiles give warmth and style to a bathroom.

'Aquarius': Heuga.

WHERE TO START

House walls are rarely built at exactly 90° to each other, however square the corners may appear. Taking one side of the room as a starting point may reduce the amount of cutting required initially, but will almost certainly leave you with an awkward – and noticeable – angle to cut across the tiles needed to fill the gap at the other side.

1 Generally the center of the room is the best place to start laying tiles. To find the center, measure along the bottom of two facing walls and mark the floor at their mid-points. Make a chalk line between the two marks, then make a mark half way along this line.

2 You now need to make a second line at right angles to this one to help you locate the correct position for your first four tiles. To do this you will need to use a home-made scriber (see page 12).

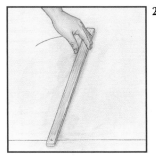

3 Place one nail on the centerpoint of your first line and scratch either side across the line. Place your scriber on each of these side-marks in turn and make two arcs.

4 Snap a chalk line between the two intersections to create your second guideline. A chalk line can be made using two pins and household string coated with chalk.

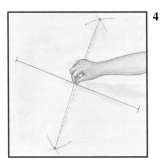

5 Dry-lay four rows of tiles from this central axis out to the four walls to check that you will not have to cut any narrow strips around the baseboards. Adjust the starting point as necessary to avoid this problem – ideally there should be at least half a tile width at each of the four edges.

6 Because you are tiling a floor rather than a wall, you have the opportunity to dry-lay as many tiles as you like before reaching for the adhesive. Any awkward projections such as built-in closets or chimney breasts should certainly be tackled 'dry' first to avoid cutting ugly, narrow tile strips.

Remember when dry-laying solid floor tiles to allow for grouting gaps as and when these are required. Check the tile manufacturer's instructions as some will recommend a minimum size.

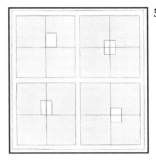

LAYING SOFT FLOOR TILES

Many soft floor tiles are self-adhesive – they have a layer of adhesive on their backs that is protected by a sheet of paper until you are ready to lay them.

With this type of tile, it is not strictly necessary to use a batten as a guide because you can just as easily follow a pencil line drawn on the floor.

Otherwise proceed as if you were laying hard floor tiles.

CUTTING SOFT FLOOR TILES

Soft floor tiles are much easier to lay than hard ones because they can be trimmed to fit around obstacles using a trimming knife or even a pair of scissors.

This will save you an enormous amount of time if you have to cut a tile to fit, say, a curve around the base of a toilet bowl or a washbasin.

LAYING HARD FLOOR TILES

1 Nail a batten along one of your starting lines, marking on it the position of the first tile before spreading a suitable adhesive over the floor.

2 Spread no more than 3sq ft of adhesive over the floor at a time. It is very important to bed tiles down before the adhesive starts to set. Use a notched trowel to spread the adhesive to improve the grip on the back of the tiles.

3 Lay three or four tiles along the batten, inserting spacers between them to make the grout gaps recommended by the tile manufacturer.

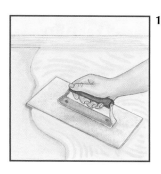

1

An 1/8in gap is suggested for most floor tiles.

4 As when hanging wall tiles, give each floor tile a twist as you lay it to remove any air pockets. Use a spirit level to check that all the tiles are bedded down evenly.

5 Now start to lay tiles at right angles to the batten, taking care to keep each row as straight as possible.

6 Keep a damp cloth handy to wipe off any adhesive that gets onto the faces of the tiles as you work.

7 When you have tiled the center of the room, spread more adhesive along one side and continue as before.

4

Most newly-laid tiles need to be left for 24 hours before they can be walked on, so you may decide to tile only one half of the room at a time if you are decorating a kitchen or bathroom that is in frequent use.

If you are keen to get the job done as quickly as possible, lay most of the whole tiles on Day One and then finish off around the edges on Day Two. Always leave yourself with an untiled walkway back to the door to avoid standing on freshly-laid tiles.

CUTTING EDGE TILES

3

A

4

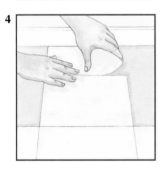

Y ou will need to use a heavy-duty tile cutter to snap floor
tiles that are to fit around the edges of the room.

It is a good idea to tackle the plain walls first before
moving onto the corners and obstacles such as doorways.

There are several techniques for accurately measuring
the gaps around the edges of the room. Using only a tape
measure is not good enough, because of the unevenness of
the walls. None of the cuts you make are likely to be square,
so it is better to adopt a measuring technique that transfers
the shape of the wall directly onto the tile that you are going
to cut.

There are two ways of doing this – the first is slightly
better suited to laying solid tiles, while either can be used
when handling soft tiles.

TECHNIQUE ONE

I f you are going to follow this method, do not fix the last
row of whole tiles in place until you have cut the edge-
tiles that will be laid next to them.

1 Dry-lay a whole tile next to the last one you have fixed
down in the row, inserting spacers for the grout gaps.

2 Lay another loose tile on top of the first, but slide this one
across to touch the wall.

3 Mark the position of this top tile's back edge with a wax
crayon or a chinagraph pencil on the loose tile below.
Take care to draw along its entire length so that when you
lift it off you are left with a clear line on the tile below.

4 Remove the tile below and place the top tile on the floor
next to the last fixed tile. Take the marked tile to your tile-
cutter.

5 If you were now to cut along the line marked on its face,
portion 'A' would exactly fit the gap left between the last
tile (as yet not fixed in place) and the wall. Because you
need to allow for grouting, you will have to mark a second
cutting line 1/8in or so back from this one, using a straight
edge (ruler) and cut along this one instead.

TECHNIQUE TWO

If you employ this cutting technique, you can lay all the whole tiles in the room before tackling the edges.

3

1 Dry-lay the tile you are going to cut neatly on top of the last fixed tile on the floor.

2 Place a second loose tile on top of this one and slide it across until it touches the wall.

3 Use a wax crayon or chinagraph pencil to mark the position of the back edge of this top tile on the face of the one you are going to cut.

4 By cutting along this line you should leave yourself with a portion of tile that exactly fits the gap.

5 Either cut along this line if you are laying soft tiles (that do not require grouting), or, if you are laying tiles that require grouting cut a $1/8$in or so back from this line to allow for the grout gap recommended by the tile manufacturer.

When fitting tiles in a corner, you can use either of the two techniques – first marking the tile along one edge and then along the other.

TILING AROUND OBSTACLES

Doorways, pipes, and the curved outlines of basin pedestals and toilet bowls will have to be carefully measured before tiles can be cut to fit around them.

A profile gauge is the tool to use for this job. The technique used to cut the tiles to size is identical to the one used to fit wall tiles around bathroom fittings (see page 29).

GROUTING FLOOR TILES

Floor tiles can be grouted using a standard cement/water mix or a product that is designed for the job. Follow the manufacturer's advice when deciding which to use.

The technique used to grout floor tiles is identical to that for grouting wall tiles (see page 23).

SAND AND CEMENT SCREEDS

If your floor is very uneven or slopes by more than 1/2in from one side of the room to the other, you will have to cover it with a sand-and-cement screed and then lay the tiles over the top.

This is not as difficult – nor as time-consuming – as it might sound, since the tiles can be laid directly onto the screed while it is still wet.

You will need to consider the fact that you will raise the level of the floor at some points by as much as 1in once the tiles have been laid. Check that the bottoms of any affected doors can be trimmed accordingly.

With a screed, tiles are laid in sections or 'bays', that are between 1/2in thick wooden battens that are fixed across the room crosswise.

To establish your starting point, you will still need to find the center of the room (see page 39) and dry-lay tiles out from this point to the walls. Adjust the rows of tiles as necessary, to avoid having to fill any narrow gaps at the edges of the room.

Next, find the highest part of the floor. At this point, the screed is going to be 1/2in thick and the rest of the floor will have to be built up to match it.

In order to be able to exit the room without stepping on any of your freshly-laid tiles, you will need to start work below the wall that is furthest from the door. Mark the position of the last full tile you have dry-laid up to this wall and then draw a line on the floor along the front edge, extending this line in both directions until it reaches the side walls.

Fix your first guide batten along this line.

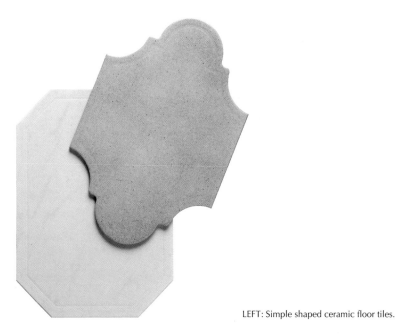

LEFT: Simple shaped ceramic floor tiles.

1 You can find the high spot using a long batten and a spirit level. Mark the spot with an offcut of wood 1/2in thick.

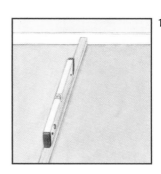

2 Mix the mortar in the ratio three parts sharp sand to one part cement. Mix it dry, then add just enough water to produce a stiff paste.

3 Spread a thin strip of mortar along your starting line and press your first batten down onto it. Stretch a spirit level between the offcut you placed at the high point of the room and this batten.

4 Adjust the height of the batten until the two are level and then level the batten itself along its own length.

If the spirit level will not stretch between the high point and the batten, tape a straight edge to it to extend its range.

5 Fix a second batten down parallel to the first, about 3ft nearer the door. Again, use the spirit level to even it up in relation to the first batten and along its own length.

6 Fill the space between the two battens with the screed, spreading it out with a steel float. A spare batten will be handy to level off the screed between the tops of the battens.

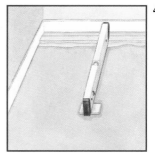

7 Mix a thin solution of cement and water (in equal parts) and pour a little over the top, then gently spread it out with your float.

8 The tiles should be laid immediately onto this mixture – tap each one down with a trowel handle. Insert spacers as you go, using your spirit level to check that you are laying the tiles horizontally.

9 When you have filled the first bay with tiles, detach the first batten from the side of the front row and re-position it 3ft behind the second to form a second bay.

Repeat the process until you have laid all the whole tiles and have reached the doorway.

You can cut and lay the edge-tiles as you go, but this is not essential. If they are going to be laid at a later date, scrape the top 1/8in off the screed before it sets and fix them in place using adhesive.

TILING A CEILING

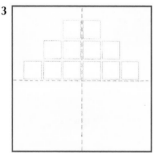

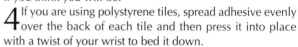

Lightweight tiles can be used to cover a ceiling that has become cracked or uneven.

Most ceiling tiles are made of polystyrene and need to be fixed in place using a special adhesive designed for this purpose. Usually sold in 12in squares, they are bevel-edged, though 24in squares are also available. The tiles are usually about 3/8in thick.

It is also possible to buy fiber tiles for ceilings. These are made from compressed mineral or wood fibers and are generally thicker than polystyrene tiles. Their edges are often tongued-and-grooved to hide the fixing pins.

Like floor tiles, ceiling tiles are always laid from the center of the room out toward the edges.

1 Find the middle of each of the four walls in the room you are decorating and insert push-pins at these points on the edges of the ceiling.

2 Fix two string lines between these pins – they will cross each other at the center of the room.

3 Dry-lay rows of tiles out from this point to the edges of the room to check that you will not be left with any awkward little gaps to fill – adjust your starting point slightly if you think you will be.

4 If you are using polystyrene tiles, spread adhesive evenly over the back of each tile and then press it into place with a twist of your wrist to bed it down.

5 Fix all the whole tiles in place before you start to trim the edge tile. This can be done with a sharp trimming knife and a steel rule.

Polystyrene tiles can be decorated with latex paints but should never be painted with oil-based paint.

Photographic props supplied by:

Nina Barough Styling

As credited, photographic material reproduced by kind permission of:

Armitage Shanks
H & R Johnson
Texas Homecare Limited
Pilkingtons Tiles
Heuga Carpet Tiles
IKEA Limited

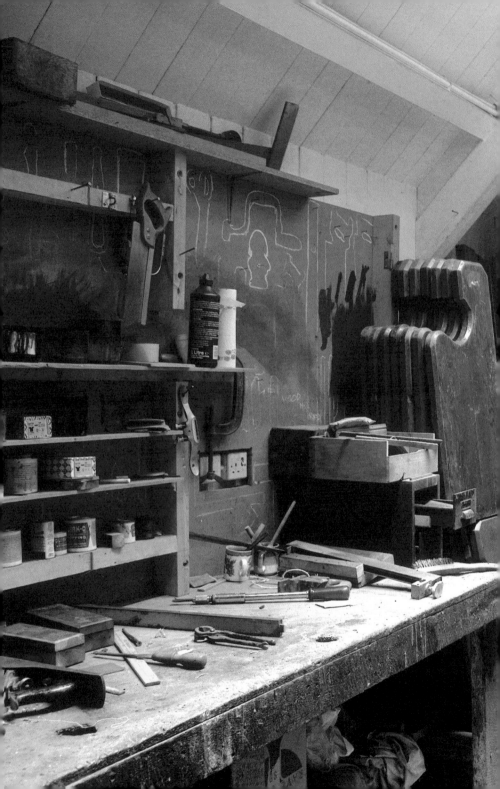